For Quinn, with love
from Auntie Jeannie xx
JW

For Emily,
my wonderful little girl
IF

First US edition 2021
First published by Nosy Crow Ltd. (UK) 2020

Library of Congress Catalog Card Number 2021931538
ISBN 978-1-5362-1733-9

TLF 25 24 23
10 9 8 7 6

Printed in Dongguan, Guangdong, China

This book was typeset in Filosofia.
The illustrations were done in mixed media.

Candlewick Press
99 Dover Street
Somerville, Massachusetts 02144

www.candlewick.com

JEANNE WILLIS
ILLUSTRATED BY ISABELLE FOLLATH

WHat ARE Little GiRLs MADE oF?

WHAT ARE LITTLE GIRLS MADE OF?

What are little girls made of?
What are little girls made of?
Sun and rain and heart and brain—
that's what girls are made of.

What are little boys made of?
What are little boys made of?
Except for little things, much the same—
that's what boys are made of.

GEORGIE PORGIE

Georgie Porgie, pudding and pie,
kissed a girl as she walked by.
"Don't kiss me unless I say!"
she said, and sent him on his way.

LITTLE JADE HORNER

Little Jade Horner
sat in a corner,
staring up at the stars.
She made little spaceships
from saucepans and hair clips
and sent all her teddies to Mars.

JACK AND JILL

Jack and Jill went up the hill
to ride their shiny scooter.
Jack fell down and lost a wheel
and bent the silver hooter.
Up Jill got and home did trot
for tools and a first-aid kit.
Now Jack is up and running
with the scooter—Jill had fixed it.

BYE, BABY BUNTING

Bye, Baby Bunting,
Mommy's gone job-hunting
to pay for a university
so you can get a good degree.

LITTLE MISS MUFFET

Little Miss Muffet
sat on a tuffet
eating her ham and eggs,
and when a big spider
then sat down beside her,
she petted his long, furry legs.

THE ITSY-BITSY SPIDER

The itsy-bitsy spider climbed up the water spout.
In came Lorraine and helped the spider out.
She put him in the garden to catch the pesky flies
and all the flowers that she grew won first prize.

No.1

No.1

No.1

No.1

LAVENDER'S BLUE

Lavender's blue, dilly dilly,
lavender's green.
You shan't be king, silly billy.
I shall be queen!

DOCTOR FOSTER

Doctor Foster went to Gloucester
in a shower of rain.
She fell in a puddle right up to her middle
and fixed the broken drain.

WHERE ARE YOU GOING TO, MY PRETTY MAID?

"Where are you going to, my pretty maid?"
"Off to school, of course," she said.
"May I go with you, my pretty maid?"
"You can if you want to, Tom," she said.
"What is your net worth, my pretty maid?"
"None of your business, Tom," she said.
"Then I can't marry you, my pretty maid."
"Nobody asked you, Tom," she said.
"And stop calling me your pretty maid!"

BONNIE SHAFTO

Bonnie Shafto's gone to sea,
silver cutlass on her knee,
fighting pirates, one, two, three.
Ahoy there, Bonnie Shafto!

Bonnie Shafto's brave and bold,
though the waves are icy cold,
and she's only six years old.
Yo-ho, Bonnie Shafto!

DIDDLE DIDDLE DUMPLING

Diddle diddle dumpling, brother John
went to bed with his night-light on,
just in case a monster came,
which ruined every nighttime game.

Diddle diddle dumpling, sister Gwen
turned the night-light off again.
"There are two monsters, it is true,"
she said, "but they are me and you!"

HUMPTY DUMPTY

Humpty Dumpty sat on a wall.
Humpty Dumpty had a great fall.
The doctor arrived
and she mended his shell
and dried all his eggy tears
gently as well.

TWINKLE, TWINKLE

"Twinkle, twinkle, little star.
  How I wonder what you are!"
"I have often wondered too,"
  said the star. "Now, who are you?"

So I answered, "I am me!"
and the star said, "Ah, I see!
I'm no longer in the dark,
as you're by far the brightest spark."

MARY, MARY

Mary, Mary, quite contrary,
always changing her style—
so sometimes she's a fairy queen,
and other times, she's a crocodile!

LITTLE BO-PEEP

Little Bo-Peep had lost her sheep.
They fell in a ditch full of slime.
She waded straight in, right up to her chin,
and rescued them one at a time.

GIRLS AND BOYS, COME OUT TO PLAY

Girls and boys, come out to play.
Kara's racing cars today.
Kai plays with a baby bear;
Sanjay's making scones to share.

Belle has built a bridge with bricks;
Kate's performing magic tricks.
Joe is wearing fancy dress—
he's a beautiful princess.

Phil and Fay pretend to fight
(Phil's a dragon, Fay's a knight).
Ray is dancing a ballet—
we play what we want to play!